*A pastel desert sky, hot white clouds, endless canyons
in layers of diminishing detail, washed in fading red tones.*

*Beneath, all as brief as the sweet breath of a desert
hummingbird, wait the sacred datura and the white-throated
swift, lizard scales and Anasazi dreams on limestone pages.*

THE GRAND CANYON

AN ARTIST'S VIEW

PAINTINGS AND DRAWINGS
JOHN D. DAWSON

STORY
CHARLES CRAIGHEAD

A Walk Through Grand Canyon National Park

PUBLISHED BY:

HAGGIS HOUSE
PUBLICATIONS, INC.
SALT LAKE CITY, UTAH

ROBERT M. PETERSEN, *Publisher*
RICHARD D. TORREY, *Editor*

RAUL TREJO, *Book Designer*

This book is published in cooperation
with Grand Canyon Association.
Special thanks to Pam Frazier and the
Grand Canyon Association for their
support and cooperation, to Greer
Price, and to the National Park Service
at Grand Canyon for preserving this
awesome landscape and all its fragile
life.

ISBN 1-881114-05-8

Printed on recycled paper in the U.S.A.

CONTENTS

Charles Craighead and Kathleen Dawson watch the sun rise over the Grand Canyon.

CONTENTS OF JOHN'S BLUE COOLER:

- Winsor Newton watercolors,
- Paints and brushes
- Liquitex paints
- Grumbacher brushes
- Linen canvas strips
- Watercolor paper
- Sketch books
- Pencils and pens
- Water

John Dawson drawing an Indian paintbrush plant, Tonto Platform, Grand Canyon.

BACKGROUND

THE first hike that John and Kathleen Dawson and I made together was in the Grand Canyon in 1984. As a writer and photographer I was used to looking at the world in a certain way, and I looked forward to showing John and Kathleen the beauty and diversity of the Grand Canyon as I knew it. It turned out that John had spent time in different parts of the park and he had an artist's perspective of the canyon. We thought our hike might turn into a disagreement over what was worth stopping to study. But we ended up having a great adventure, each of us inspired by the others, and we saw and experienced things we never would have found hiking alone.

John and Kathleen work as a team. Her insight and quiet persuasion always steer John back on track when he strays too far into his artist's world of insect parts, flowers and birds. She also has a great eye for color and helps John match the subtle natural shades of birds and wildflowers.

The only problem with hiking with John is that we never get very far down the trail; he always finds something really interesting to draw and we can't help looking over his shoulder as his work takes shape. For my part I try to push him a little farther down the trail to see places I know he'll like, and I tell him stories that weave around our day's discoveries.

After every hike we would sit in the evening and look at John's sketchbook. It would be filled with his drawings, half-finished watercolors and notes, and along the borders would be penciled some of the stories and ideas I had told him. It would look suspiciously like the start of a book, and we began to dream about collaborating on a real book. From fly fishing in Yellowstone National Park to watching mountain lions in Idaho, the book was always on our minds: A Walk with an Artist. John began sending our ideas to his long-time friend, artist and designer Raul Trejo, and he would create beautiful sample pages of our book to encourage us on.

When John called and said that he and Kathleen were going to be spending a week on the South Rim of the Grand Canyon it seemed like a perfect chance for some Dawson-style hiking. Then John called back to say that his publisher friend, Bob Petersen, was interested in our dream book if it was done on the Grand Canyon. Raul joined us and we all headed for the South Rim. We decided from the start to let the natural spontaneity of our old hikes try to come out. Once we started down the trail everything fell into place. I hope this book reflects both the spirit and the substance of taking a walk in the Grand Canyon with my favorite natural history artist.

C.C.

An Artist's View...5

GUIDO FRICK

"The Barn at the Base" o/c 18" x 24"

"Resting in the Woods" o/c 24" x 30"

NEXT WORKSHOPS:

ROCIADA, NEW MEXICO June 8th - 12th Fredericksburg Artists' School
AMARILLO, TEXAS June 15th - 17th Amarillo Art Institute

Now Available: Two CDs (DVD) with demonstration by Guido Frick painting a still life and a landscape.
Runs more than 2 hours. Cost: $140 (S&H Incl.)

FOR DVD-ORDER AND/OR WORKSHOP INFO, PLEASE CONTACT FRICKARTIST@AOL.COM
See also WWW.GUIDOFRICK.COM and WWW.GUIDOFRICK.DE

EDWARD ALDRICH

Edward Aldrich | Survivor | 34" x 34" | Oil on linen

EVERGREEN FINE ART
Gallery & Sculpture Garden

3042 Evergreen Parkway | Evergreen, Colorado 80439
303.679.3610 | 800.452.9453 | evergreenfineart.com

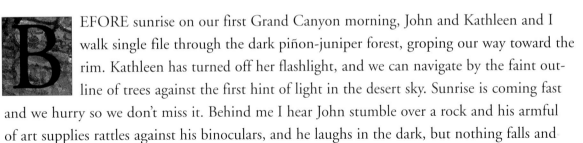

THE RIM

BEFORE sunrise on our first Grand Canyon morning, John and Kathleen and I walk single file through the dark piñon-juniper forest, groping our way toward the rim. Kathleen has turned off her flashlight, and we can navigate by the faint outline of trees against the first hint of light in the desert sky. Sunrise is coming fast and we hurry so we don't miss it. Behind me I hear John stumble over a rock and his armful of art supplies rattles against his binoculars, and he laughs in the dark, but nothing falls and we go on. The first intense colors of sunrise will fade quickly and John wants to get them etched firmly in his mind, both for reference and for inspiration. At first we whispered as we walked, but now we are silent, listening for the clear sounds surrounding desert sunrise.

Soft pine needles under our feet give way to hard, bare ground and then to rock, and we can see a great, shadowy void just beyond the last gnarled trees. The canyon's great expanse seems to absorb all light and color at this early hour. We pick our way around crumbling rocks to reach the edge. When we finally step past the last wind-carved piñon pines and confront the Grand Canyon, it's the same feeling of immensity as walking out under a brilliant night sky or seeing the ocean for the first time. There's a tinge of deep red low in the east now and just enough light is filtering down into the canyon to outline the far rim and reveal the features below.

The first bird of the day sings once from somewhere back in the trees. A house finch? The air is perfectly still, almost like the canyon is holding its breath for a minute before another day begins. We just stand and stare as particle by particle the Grand Canyon seems to materialize out of the dark. John recovers first from our awe and scrambles for a flat rock where he can sit with his feet dangling over the edge. Morning light is bouncing everywhere now but in the deepest shadows below, and the rich reds of sunrise have touched the high points on the north horizon across the canyon from us.

Kathleen and I can hear John laying out his watercolors and opening his sketchbook, so we go sit beside him. John's pencil is already busy and the first angular lines of the Grand Canyon are taking shape on his paper. I just sit and watch the canyon's subtle changes in light and color. A pair of ravens flies by, beating their wings in the still air, going somewhere in a hurry, as if late for work.

Several mule deer move out into the early AM light

8...*The Grand Canyon*

We sit among the rocks out on a small point of the rim, one of many where the scalloped edge of the rim curves in and out to form a series of amphitheaters. Across from us on the next point we see several gray forms begin to move, and as they come out into the light they take shape as mule deer. They had been motionless, watching us stumble around until they determined we were harmless. Almost as soon as the deer move, a gray-and-blonde coyote appears from the cliffrose where it was watching and trots along the rim between us and the deer. The coyote's nose is to the ground as it glides down the trail. It stops and starts, turns and sniffs, and at one point looks down into the canyon and cocks its ears. What can it hear and see way down there?

An Artist's View...9

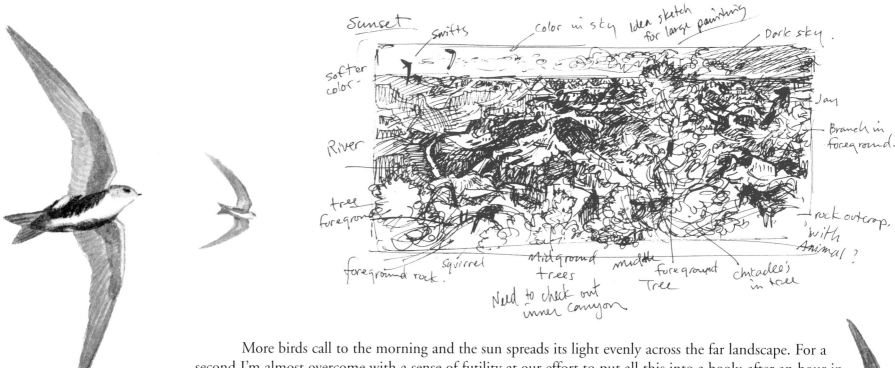

The vivid colors of sunrise begin to fade, and when John settles in to the slow process of filling in the details of his painting, Kathleen and I abandon him to his work and wander off to explore the rest of the point. We find a spot with a view to the west and sit for a minute with our backs to a square block of Kaibab Limestone. The sun is full above the horizon behind us and the day begins. A small fence lizard tiptoes out into the sun to warm itself. A few minutes later John finds us, and we all sit under a piñon pine and soak up the early sunshine.

white-throated swift

More birds call to the morning and the sun spreads its light evenly across the far landscape. For a second I'm almost overcome with a sense of futility at our effort to put all this into a book; after an hour in this beauty my crisp new journal is still blank and my favorite pencil is in my pocket. But the day is fresh and it's a peaceful guilt.

I try to tell them about my lack of words and empty pages, and John laughs and says, "Look at this. I'm not sure where to start, either." He shows us a sketch that tapers off into white paper. "What do you think?" he asks us.

I say, "Maybe we're trying to capture too much too fast. I think we just need to sit and watch for a while."

It's warm and quiet sitting here, except for a soft breeze that begins to breathe out of the canyon. Sunlight is reaching farther down into the canyon and it warms the air, and in the new currents a white-throated swift races past us. Another follows close behind, sailing by just a few feet over our heads, and they skim along the rim at what seems like a hundred miles an hour. With their long, pointed wings arcing back the swifts look like little tightly-strung bows flying through the air. They seldom flap their wings, and then it is just a brief flicker and

A cliff chipmunk scurries past us and disappears over the edge. A minute later it pops up and scampers into a bunch of cliffrose. It runs back and forth over the rim with seeds or grass in its cheeks. We realize that the rocky edge we perceive as the brink of a huge canyon is just another rock to the chipmunk.

C.L.

Golden Eagle

they sail off even faster. They race back and forth in front of us and then vanish in a second.

John sketches the swifts and I'm thumbing through my bird book to make sure what kind we've just seen when Kathleen says, "What kind of bird is that?"

She's looking with binoculars back over the piñon-juniper forest to the south. The bird is soaring, hawk-like, in broad circles. John takes the binoculars and looks, and then starts sketching without telling us what it is. He alternates looking through his binoculars and down at his sketchbook as he works and the bird takes form: a golden eagle. This could be a fun game, where John looks at a distant thing and draws, and we try to guess what it is. The eagle circles higher and wider and follows the wind back over the forest out of sight. We turn our attention back to the canyon. The full, fresh morning light is illuminating the canyon perfectly right now, and John begins drawing the view, the structure of the ridges and cliffs and layers of rock that make up the scene.

As he works, John tells us what had been troubling him earlier while he was trying to capture both the shape and the detail of the canyon at first light. He's used to knowing what he's drawing, knowing the texture of bird feathers or the feel of lizard skin. If he draws a piñon pine into a scene he knows it has two needles in a bundle, the cones are egg-shaped with thick scales, and the nuts are delicious. Here in the Grand Canyon he can see this beautiful vista and he can duplicate it on paper, but he doesn't have a real feel for all the elements. He shows us his first drawing and he starts putting arrows and questions around the edges. What plant makes this area gray-green? What are those bright yellow-green specks down here? What lives here, in these trees? What's inside this crevice? How big is everything in proportion?

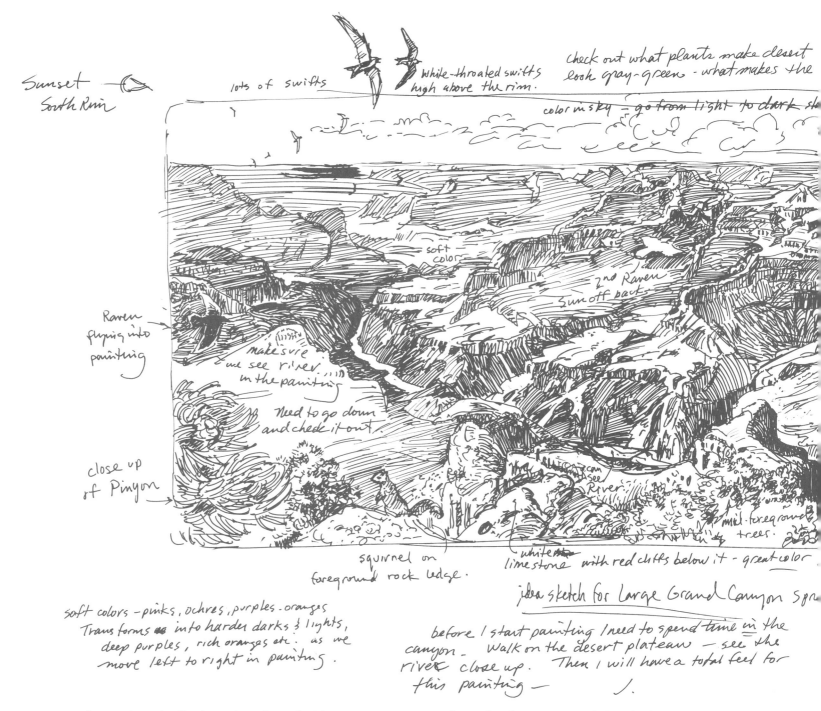

Sunset →
South Rim

lots of swifts

white-throated swifts
high above the rim.

check out what plants make desert
look gray-green - what makes the

color in sky - go from light to dark sk

soft color

2nd Raven
Sun off back.

Raven flying into painting

make sure we see river in the painting

Need to go down and check it out.

close up of Pinyon

can see River

mid. foreground trees.

squirrel on foreground rock ledge.

white
limestone with red cliffs below it - great color

idea sketch for Large Grand Canyon spr

soft colors - pinks, ochres, purples. oranges
Transforms into harder darks & lights,
deep purples, rich oranges etc. as we
move left to right in painting.

before I start painting I need to spend time in the
canyon - Walk on the desert plateau — see the
river close up. Then I will have a total feel for
this painting —

So we sit and talk about it and we decide to go on a treasure hunt for the texture and detail of the Grand Canyon. Obviously we won't see everything, but we should find enough to make John feel comfortable in his work. First we'll explore the South Rim with its vistas and forests, then we'll hike down into the canyon to the Colorado River. It will be a typical Dawson hike, stopping to look at everything from flowers to snakes, lots of drawing and quick watercolors. Kathleen and I look at each other and she rolls her eyes. It's difficult to get John more than a few miles down the trail

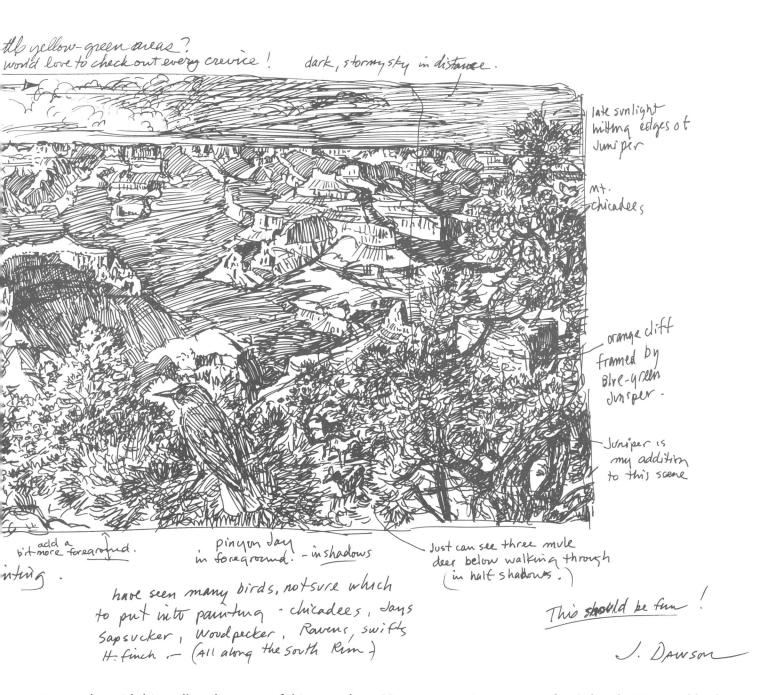

the yellow-green areas?
would love to check out every crevice! dark, stormy sky in distance.

late sunlight
hitting edges of
Juniper

Mt.
chicadees

orange cliff
framed by
Blue-green
Juniper.

Juniper is
my addition
to this scene

add a
bit more foreground.

pinyon Jay
in foreground. - in shadows

Just can see three mule
deer below walking through
(in half shadows.)

inting.

have seen many birds, not sure which
to put into painting - chicadees, Jays
Sapsucker, Woodpecker, Ravens, swifts
H. finch. - (All along the South Rim)

This should be fun!

J. Dawson

in one day with his endless discovery of things to draw. How are we going to get to the Colorado River and back?

As if he can read our thoughts John laughs and says, "I promise to be selective. No turning over rocks or poking into rotten logs. This will be the Grand Canyon just as we find it." We'll begin by walking along the rim and winding through the pine forests behind us. John will draw and I'll make notes and Kathleen will get us home by dark.

The peregrine is a specialist, a predator balanced at the top of a diverse natural world. Its presence in the Canyon indicates things must be somewhat in order.

C.C.

After we finish our breakfast of sandwiches and fruit and water we all sort of doze in the warm sun for a few minutes. No one is in a hurry. This is nice, closing our eyes and listening: wind over the rocks, the chatter of swallows and swifts out over the canyon, wind in the cliffrose and twisted piñon pines clinging to the edge, an occasional call of a jay or woodpecker back in the trees, the almost hollow sound a canyon brings to the land. I'm nearly lulled to sleep when I hear something from deep in the canyon, rising up on the soft wind: the harsh, almost nasal cry of a peregrine falcon. We all sit up and let our eyes sweep over the canyon, looking for a dark, fast moving bird. Drifting up out of the canyon depths on a thermal updraft, the falcon soars in tight circles until it reaches a prominent rock on a ridge below us, where it lands. It cries a few times and then settles down, watching the canyon skies intently. We notice there are suddenly no swifts or swallows in the air around us. They all disappeared when the falcon arrived. Peregrines can catch these birds in the air, but this one doesn't seem to be hunting.

May be as many as a pair of peregrines every five miles of the Colorado River in Grand Canyon. Main prey is white-throated swifts here. How fast does a peregrine have to be to catch a swift in mid-air? Have also been observed in Grand Canyon catching bats.

C.C.

Besides being a rare and exciting find for us, the presence of a peregrine falcon reminds us we are in wild and undisturbed country. While we watch, the peregrine lifts its wings and effortlessly catches the canyon wind. It circles the rock once, turns downwind and is gone.

An Artist's View...15

The three of us start walking along the rim, weaving in and out of the piñon-juniper forest as we follow the eroded contours of the canyon. The forest looks almost like it was pushed to the edge, where a last line of weathered trees clings to exposed rock. Scattered individual trees have taken root in crevices and on ledges in the canyon below. At each opportunity we peer over the edge. Limestone, sandstone, shale, limestone, sandstone, granite…all layered below us in a broad sweep of exposed earth.

When we leave the open brink and shortcut across promontories we have to wind our way through the forest of rounded, bushy piñon and juniper trees. They all stand a little way apart from each other and leave the forest floor open, without much else growing there. The ground is covered with a mix of pine needles, juniper berries and pine cones. There are chunks of Kaibab Limestone and old tree trunks and broken, weathered limbs. This is John's kind of place, where he could spend hours on his hands and knees exploring and drawing the forest elements. He jumps from one spot to another as he sketches pine cones, needles and trees. Kathleen stays ahead of John looking for interesting things to try to lure him ahead at a reasonable pace. I look for birds in the dense treetops.

Scattered throughout the pinon-juniper forest we keep finding small stands of Gambel oak trees, small scrubby-looking oaks. We first see a few oak leaves looking out of place on the bed of pine needles, then we follow the trail of leaves until we come upon a dense little stand of oaks. The ground is littered with old acorns. Most of them are chewed or pecked open and the nutritious contents eaten. Many of the opened acorns are ringed with the tiny toothmarks of mice or squirrels, and we can see deer tracks in the bare ground under the trees.

Oak galls caused often by insects like gall wasps or aphids, fungus or disease. Can't tell what formed these. J.

Kaibab limestone

16…The Grand Canyon

mistletoe
on juniper

8X up.

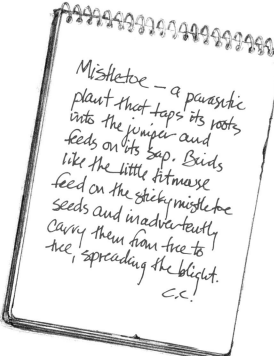

Mistletoe — a parasitic plant that taps its roots into the juniper and feeds on its sap. Birds like the little titmouse feed on the sticky mistletoe seeds and inadvertently carry them from tree to tree, spreading the blight.
C.C.

I see a flash of gray up high in one of the junipers and start following it, trying to see the little bird that's darting in and out of sight in the bundles of needles. After a few minutes of waiting I see the bird work its way around the tree to my side. At first all I can see is a small gray body, and then the head comes into view and I can see a gray crest. It's a plain titmouse, much prettier than its bland name suggests. I whistle to the others and they get a quick look before the titmouse flies off. At times like this I envy John's artistic abilities; my photograph will show only the rear end of an indistinct gray bird half hidden in the juniper needles, but with the same glimpse of the bird John will produce a perfect likeness of the delicate little titmouse.

While we're all looking up into the trees Kathleen comments on the clusters of contrasting light green growth we see randomly throughout the juniper trees. I bend a low limb down and we take a close look at one of the clusters. At first it appears to be slightly deformed juniper needles, pale green and scaly, but it has its own little flowers. This is mistletoe.

An Artist's View...17

Close to the Grand Canyon's edge the soil gets thin, exposing more of the canyon's top layer of Kaibab Limestone. The ground is dry and vegetation is sparse, but bursting out of a thin bed of juniper needles and framed by crumbling rock is a claretcup hedgehog cactus in full bloom. The claretcup has a dozen spiny stems and half that many intense red blossoms. In contrast to the drab greens, browns and grays of the piñon-juniper forest, the claretcup is almost jewel-like. We walk completely around the plant, drinking in the rich colors from all sides. The hue of the petals changes subtly as we see them in different angles of sunlight. We sit for a while and John draws the cactus and mixes his paints to try to match the claretcup colors. I'm always amazed to see him brushing little puddles of paint around until the perfect color appears and he puts it on paper. With the claretcup hedgehog safely duplicated in his sketchbook we move on.

claretcup cactus
along south rim
in cloud shadow

The bare trunk of an old juniper lies on the ground, framed by gnarled limbs and with the deep shadows of the vast Grand Canyon for a backdrop. Sunlight filters through the branches of surrounding trees to spotlight the log. John is standing and staring at the scene. He turns to us and says, "Isn't this the perfect spot for a cougar? I'm really tempted to do a painting here."

Kathleen shrugs. She's heard this before, whenever John is torn between sticking to the facts and using artistic license. Because much of the animal life here is nocturnal or elusive we see more signs than actual animals, so John says "This can be one of my 'What if' pieces," and he sits down to draw the juniper log with a big cat prowling past.

We know there are cougars here on the South Rim even though we don't expect to see one. Most are on the North Rim. When John finishes he looks at it for a minute and then pencils in "What if" below. He photographs all the details of the log and its setting to do a complete painting later in his studio, and we go on.

what if ....
I can just imagine a
cougar walking by ..
what a great spot !

Ravens are one of the few birds that appear to fly just for enjoyment...diving, rolling, chasing one another. Often seek unusual air currents. Have watched them play for hours in powerful updraft wind, flying into it over and over to be tossed and tumbled about, cawing loudly each time.

cc.

Ravens are both scavengers and hunters...very intelligent and adaptable with amazing flying abilities.

cc.

The first thing we notice when we break out of the trees is the strong afternoon wind. Back in the forest it was just a steady background noise in the treetops, but now we step right out into it. When we have to bend over into a sudden wind gust we understand how a tree hanging on the edge of the canyon in this wind would weather and twist and curl its bark. But with the wind there is also a great feeling of freedom and space. When we walk out of the piñon pines and juniper trees, where we could only see a few hundred feet ahead, and stand on the edge of the canyon where the horizon is suddenly miles away, we all take a deep breath and spread our arms like wings in the wind.

We are answered by three ravens. They tumble out of the sky from the east, playing in the wind and calling loudly. The swirling air currents buffet the ravens as they dive and climb and chase each other in some game of raven tag. Ravens, dry canyon wind, a small band of humans on a rock; it all feels so timeless. Ravens have been with mankind since we first walked the earth. Ancient European cave paintings depict ravens perched around camp 14,000 years ago, and here in the Grand Canyon the Anasazi and ancient ravens must surely have mingled. Now the three of us sit on the rim with our own generations of ravens. Beneath the wind and raven calls I can hear John's pen scratching away, bringing the birds to life on paper.

We find a seat on the edge of the cliffs under a wind-sculptured pine. We have an unobstructed view of the canyon, while a thick jumble of cliffrose and Mormon tea blocks the worst of the wind. For the moment this is the perfect balance of warm sunshine and cool wind, so we decide to sit for a while and watch for ravens, swifts and other wind-loving birds. We eat a late lunch of nuts and cheese and crackers and a pleasant hour passes while we hide from the wind and trade raven stories.

When the afternoon shadows begin stretching across the canyon we pack up and follow an old trail where it winds off through the trees. During snowmelt in spring or after heavy summer rains the trail becomes a stream of muddy red-brown water, carrying along a flood of pine cones and needles and twigs. It makes a path of bare ground through the needles and leaves of the forest floor and we hope it will reveal tracks or other signs of life as we walk along it. There was a hard rain a few days ago, and there are piles of leaves and needles and tree bark, like little logjams, at each bend in the trail where the rushing water washed the debris. It looks as if the water was four or five inches deep in the trail. Now, in the smooth, damp ground we begin to see tracks.

We find where a mule deer crossed the trail and where some kind of rodent, maybe a squirrel, raced across the wet ground and left indistinct tracks. We almost miss the next tracks, of an elk, set deep in the mud but camouflaged by pine needles and leaves. Farther on there are tracks of three or four more elk coming off the ridge to the left and onto the trail, where they merge and go on. It looks like the animals were walking single file once they reached the trail, headed off for water or food somewhere.

A little farther down the trail coyote tracks join in and seem to follow the elk tracks. We make up various stories about what could have happened. Is the coyote really following the elk or is this just a convenient trail? Our guess is that the coyote will follow anything for a while to see if there's a chance of food. This could even be the same coyote we saw on the rim this morning. We find a weather-bleached old coyote scat consisting mostly of hair and small bones, probably of mice, so maybe this trail is a regular haunt for the coyote.

idea sketch for gray fox painting   J. DAWSON '95

Kathleen finds a set of smaller tracks crossing the trail. They look like small coyote tracks, and we decide they might have been made by a gray fox. These foxes are mostly nocturnal, smaller than coyotes, and they live in wooded and rocky areas, which is exactly where we are now. Gray foxes can climb trees fairly well, and it's easy to picture a fox up in one of these shaggy, low-limbed junipers or piñon pines. We take photographs of tracks and trees and the trail winding off down the hill. At times like this when there isn't an immediate need to draw, and the finished painting will be detailed, John takes photographs to use for reference later in his studio. He thinks he will paint the gray fox on the ground, where we saw its prints.

When we skirt around a muddy spot in the trail and have to veer into the trees, I see a familiar looking pile of coarse sand and tiny pebbles: an ant hill. Normally I'd probably ignore an ant hill in my walks, but I know this will interest John, especially since it is a perfect example of animal life re-shaping the Grand Canyon landscape bit by tiny bit. These ants look dark red to me. John looks at them and says they're harvester ants. He's painted them before, and

I am sure these are the same species of Harvester ant, (pogonomyrmex rugosus) that I did paintings of for a June, 1984 National Geographic magazine article by Bert Hölldobler,

grooves

workers

head about same size as gaster

Actual size

long hair

back leg longer

he tells us how the workers go out only during the day to gather bits of vegetation and bring it back to the nest. He reminds us that their sting is extremely painful, and Kathleen and I immediately step back and check our shoes and pantlegs for stray ants. John must have learned something from painting ants before, because now he sits down next to the ant hill to draw them and they seem to ignore him. Kathleen and I agree this is the way to study biting ants...by looking at the sketchbook.

While John draws he tells us, "The naturalist E.O. Wilson said something like the mass of all the ants and the mass of all the humans on earth are about the same. That's a lot of ants." We agree, but then I think of the Grand Canyon's dimensions and know that ants and humans together wouldn't begin to fill a corner of the canyon's vast space. But I can picture billions of ants creating the canyon by hauling out a grain at a time, laboring tirelessly for eons. Erosion probably worked at about the same ant's pace.

Within a few hundred feet of the ant hill the piñon-juniper forest changes and we begin to see a few stately ponderosa pines, and before we know it we are walking in a beautiful, open forest. Our muddy trail spreads out and disappears beneath a bed of long, soft ponderosa needles. The ground is littered with cones and little jigsaw puzzle pieces of bark. It's a fascinating change from the low, shrubby piñon and juniper trees to these ponderosa pines, like walking into a different room and closing the door behind you. They are tall and straight, with no limbs on the lower part of their massive trunks, and the trees are spaced far apart. It's almost cathedral-like here, open below with a canopy of soft green needles high overhead, with the late afternoon rays of sun and the hushed sounds.

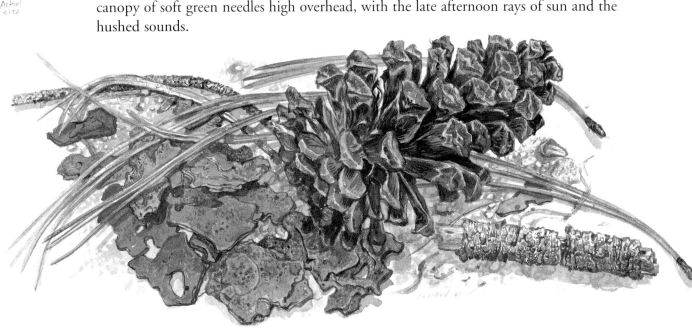

Pygmy
Nuthatcha

White breasted
Nuthatch

Nuthatches are permanent
residents on rim and most
common bird in ponderosa
Pines. Work down
tree trunk or
along limbs,
probing for
insects in
rough bark.

white-breasted is
largest Nuthatch in area.

Pygmy
Nuthatch

Ponderosa pine is
dominant tree here in
Transition Zone, between
Upper Sonoran Zone below
us and Boreal Zone up higher.
Not much understory for birds
other than tree dwellers like
nuthatches, woodpeckers and
Creepers.

J. DAWSON

Brown Creeper
works upward on
tree as it spirals
around trunk. Probes
for insects in bark.
Often nests by stuffing nest
material under slab of loose
bark on dead tree.

The wind is just a gentle whisper up in the treetops. We see a woodpecker and a couple of small birds that disappear around the massive tree trunks as we approach, so we sit down for a bit to watch and see if they will come back out. Within minutes the forest comes alive with bird calls and activity. The ponderosa pines are in various stages of life, from healthy young trees to standing dead snags. Everywhere we look there are holes and hollows. This looks like bird heaven.

We sit facing two or three big trees and wait to see what happens. On the ground I can see several places where pocket gophers have pushed mounds of red soil up through the blanket of pine needles, and I wonder how many other rodents and small animals are hidden in the forest. There are at least shrews and mice and squirrels hidden here somewhere. If there are mice, there must also be predators like weasels and owls. John nudges me out of my thoughts and points quietly to a nearby tree where a nuthatch is working its way down the trunk. The tree is dead, and big slabs of the rough bark have come loose and peeled away from the trunk. The nuthatch works around the tree until it's partway under the bottom edge of a piece of bark, and starts chipping away at a small hole, trying to widen it and hollow out a nesting site. Kathleen passes John her binoculars and an open bird book. She points to the illustration of the pygmy nuthatch and smiles. The nuthatch flies off to look at another tree and calls from there. Its voice sounds like a little rubber toy being squeezed.

At the base of the same tree we see a flash of brown and a tiny brown creeper starts working around the tree, spiralling upward and probing in crevices in the bark for insects. The rough ponderosa bark looks perfect for this kind of bird. The creeper flies off to another tree, landing at the base and spiralling upwards again.

Woodpeckers call and rattle on dead limbs and the trees are in constant motion with little birds. Sitting here in this dynamic forest it's hard to think of the open, deserty space of the Grand Canyon less than a mile away. We feel isolated from the canyon in this comfortable little glade, and John and Kathleen and I talk over our plans to hike down in the hot canyon and see what makes up the next zone. John says he has a good feel for the life along the rim, how the landscape rises up out of the desert to reach this relatively cool and moist altitude where pine trees can grow. The nearby cliff edge is an area of abrupt transition. There are some animals, like the raven and coyote, that move easily back and forth over the lip of the rim, and there are others, like owls and squirrels of this forest, that will never venture over the edge. A few desert plants from down below survive on the rim and some of the rim's vegetation has found a toehold partway down into the canyon, but for the most part they are distinctly different places.

The red-shafted flicker is named for the color of its feathers' shafts. Common along the rim — loud and not at all secretive. Yellow-shafted flicker is a rare Eastern visitor.

CL.

We sit in the ponderosa pine forest until the light begins to fade and the last few songbirds call and settle in for the night. We all wish we had perfect night vision so we could watch the forest come to life. All the tracks and animal sign we have seen tell us there is lots more going on than we will ever see. The wind is gone from the treetops and we can hear muted rustling here and there. We realize the time has slipped away and it's suddenly getting very dark. The moon won't be up for a while so Kathleen takes out her flashlight and we start walking. We try not to think of mountain lions or bears watching us from the darkness.

The day is a jumble in my mind and my journal is a mess. Early this morning I was thinking simply of the Grand Canyon as eroded outlines of red rock framed by desert air. Rock and air. Now I have to surround that image with a forest full of deer, coyotes, elk, birds, rodents, flowers and lots of ants. The canyon is not complete without its cloaking forest.

John stops us and has us listen for something he hears off in the trees. It comes again, the soft hooting of an owl. We start naming owls common to this area. It's definitely too soft for a great horned owl, and not the whistling call of the western screech owl. When we hear a second owl answer from closer to us we think it might be a pair of flammulated owls. They're summer residents and nest in old woodpecker holes in open pine forest, exactly the kind of habitat we're in. I try to make a mimicing hoot back to get them to answer and come closer, but it's a poor imitation and we all start laughing, and the owls stop calling to each other. A minute later we hear them again from far off in the ponderosa pines.

As we leave the darkened forest we think about our search for details of the Grand Canyon landscape. John is carrying a sketchbook full of South Rim paintings, drawings and notes. Tomorrow we'll go around to the North Rim, to walk in its quiet and cool spaces and search for another perspective on the canyon. After that we'll return to the South Rim, load our backpacks with paint and brushes, and descend into the canyon.

The tiny flammulated owl is about the same size as a large Ponderosa pine cone. No wonder we didn't see them. J.

THE NORTH RIM

IN a place of such immense space and sheer mass of exposed earth, it's funny that comparisons between the North Rim and the South Rim of the Grand Canyon often come down to two squirrels. While it's hard to comprehend the geologic and climatic changes that have occurred here, we can relate to the lifespan of a small squirrel and how that can be used as a measure of time and distance. Forces that can take the sand of an ancient sea and turn it into rocks in a desert are much beyond the human time scale. We can better understand the time it takes to divide a population of squirrels into two groups and then for one of those groups to evolve into a different-looking squirrel.

When the Grand Canyon area gradually dried out and warmed up thousands of years ago from a cool, forest-supporting climate to a more desertlike landscape, the once vast forests slowly died off in the lower and warmer locations. The Kaibab Plateau on the North Rim became a high, cool island of trees, and the squirrels living there were cut off by desert from the other squirrels in other forests. Certain physical traits began to emerge as genetic mixing tapered off, and eventually a distinct sub-species was running through the treetops of the North Rim. Their behavior and life cycles were the same, but the new Kaibab squirrels had a flashy white tail and a dark, charcoal-colored body. During all this time of squirrel evolution the rocks of the Grand Canyon remained the same.

PERCEPTIONS

When viewed from the south, the North Rim appears as a remote and impossibly distant place. Even though the cool glades and deep forests are only a small part of the north side, it is there that we look. The gulf of desert air between north and south rims distorts the perception of distance and magnifies the illusion of size. We can look down into the canyon and chart a path through the maze of eroded rock and follow it up to the other rim. In some ways it would be nice if the only path to the oasis high on the Kaibab Plateau was by that arduous trail down and across the canyon.

The North Rim would make a perfect remote kingdom. Imagine a fur-cloaked king and queen in their limestone castle set in the massive ponderosa pines and looking out over the canyon. There would be stables of long-haired ponies, giant cats prowling the forests and long winters of telling tales by the fire in a great hall. Guests who made the long trek across the canyon would be given rooms and made welcome to feast on roasted deer and drink the local beer brewed from pine nuts and juniper berries.

When John and Kathleen and I wander around on the North Rim the illusions vanish but there remains a difference. The air is clean and cool, and the wind that pushes against the ponderosa pines seems to be pitched a notch higher. Although we stand on the same Kaibab Limestone as on the South Rim, the ground has a new feel to it. Here and there are telltale signs of the deep winter snows, signs like shrubs that grow low and flattened to the ground and limbs broken and bent from the weight of winter. Here the nuthatches and brown creepers seem to move a little quicker.

We find it easier to be alone with our work here on the North Rim. It's not so much the changes in vegetation or temperature or the lack of tourists, but the more intangible feeling of being in the company of a Kaibab squirrel and maybe a Lewis' woodpecker. The wind seems to hush rather than to stir up distant sounds and smells, and the sunlight that filters down through the pines is a bit purer and cooler. Here the passage of great amounts of time is more real. The North Rim seems to say to us: This is what's left after all that geologic and climatic history, and it could disappear in a lifetime, so breathe this air deeply and remember the smell of these forests.

sketch from North Rim Trail

Hairy Woodpecker
just flew by

J. Dawson

A Dry Palette

THE INNER CANYON

WE'VE been sitting since first light on a big, tilted slab of sandstone, watching for the few visible inhabitants of the inner canyon before the heat sends them into hiding for the day. Our feet are on slickrock, where a seasonal flow of water has worn a smooth, bowl-like channel just before dropping off the edge of a low cliff to disappear into the dry rocks and brush below us. During a rainstorm this is probably a fifty-foot waterfall, but now the rock and everything around it is dry, including us. Off a ways from us at the base of the cliff is a little patch of lush, bright green vegetation where water is seeping out of the desert rock to make a little oasis.

Off to our right, the rock outcropping we're sitting on curves away around the contours of the land. In the narrow band of vegetation between layers of exposed rock a small band of desert bighorn sheep is slowly moving along in our direction. John is scribbling furiously. There are five sheep and they move one or two at a time, sort of leap-frogging each other along the ledge, eating, pausing and watching, going on. They seem to be finding lots of grass in the scrubby desert vegetation. It looks to us like they are making their way from the seep down below to spend the day up in a shaded side canyon behind us.

A pair of black-tailed gnatcatchers, small wren-like birds with black heads and black tails, flit around us. They fly endlessly back and forth between an agave stalk, a dead mesquite tree and a rock, flirting with each other. Sometimes one will hover like a flycatcher around a big blackbrush. John adds them to the drawing of the sheep.

A small lizard rustles through the dry leaves at the base of a flower and cocks its head to peer over at us with one eye. John flips his page over and sketches the lizard while it appears to wait patiently. When he finishes and we turn back to see what the bighorn sheep are doing, they are gone, out of sight behind the rise of a small ridge leading up toward the rim.

yellow backed spiny lizard

An Artist's View...31

Desert phlox

Rock squirrel along the trail

Sunlight reaches over the rim to touch our camp and within minutes the temperature climbs dramatically. Bird songs cease in the new heat. Soft echoes of a rock clattering downhill come from the shaded ledges where the sheep are bedding down for the day. We're definitely in the heart of the Grand Canyon. As the sun arcs higher, colors in the canyon's vermilion rocks wash out and fade in the intense desert light. Terms like "furnace" and "oven" come to mind.

High above us on the rim the band of piñon pines looks green and invitingly cool. Our packs are heavily loaded with non-essential things like paints, binoculars, cameras, sketchbooks and field guides. How did we talk ourselves into this?

THE DAY BEFORE: We begin our descent into the Grand Canyon at dawn. For the first hour we go deeper and deeper a step at a time, watching our perspective change with each bend in the trail. It's fascinating how the view of such an immense place can change within a few feet. The erosion and weathering patterns are striking; alternating hard and soft layers of rock form pillars, ridges, cliffs, slopes and precariously balanced rock sculptures. We can look down and see the trail winding along below us and we begin to anticipate the changes that lie ahead. At each new rock layer we encounter we remind ourselves of what it once was: ancient sea, ancient sea, desert, swamp, sea. The canyon is a storyboard of the earth.

The scene is so spectacular and the colors so rich, the shadows and highlights so dramatic, I have the feeling we're walking into a huge painting. It's like we're examining a great master's work, except that we're able to enter the painting to peer at all the brushstrokes and dabs of color to see how it was done. John is making notes of the various colors and textures we see and what creates them. After our first day when John was constantly taking his backpack off to get things, he now carries his notes and art materials conveniently in a plastic cooler, which wouldn't be socially acceptable for a well-outfitted hiker, but for some reason is appropriate for an artist. But it does draw some envious looks from parched backpackers on the trail who assume it's full of ice and cold drinks. Kathleen quits trying to apologize for the ugly cooler, just shrugs her shoulders and lets John explain.

We begin to see delicate wildflowers growing in pockets eroded in the rock where water collects, like little vases. A rock squirrel runs across the trail and bounds over the rocks until it reaches a safe perch in a big boulder, and we start to concentrate more on our search. We watch a delicate, little orange-tipped butterfly float across in front of us and out over the steep slope of the canyon, and it makes us feel confined here on the ground. We wonder how much we're missing by not being able to fly. John draws a collared lizard that clings to a rock by the trail. The lizard is sitting on a piece of Coconino Sandstone, a rock layer full of fossilized lizard tracks from prehistoric times, and I think of all the millions of lizards like this one that have lived and died without leaving any tracks.

An Artist's View…33

rock in the fork of a piñon

I look at my own bootprints mingled with countless others on the trail. They look nothing like human feet. It makes me want to stamp a perfect footprint somewhere and carefully cover it with sand, making a deliberate fossil of my own brief time in the canyon.

We all walk quietly for a ways, reaching out to touch the changing rock layers and thinking about the passage of time. A raven accompanies us, wheeling slowly around and around in the hot sky. The tenacity of life is fascinating, surviving all the eons of geologic changes we see reflected in the exposed layers. Kathleen points out an interesting thing relating to these thoughts: a rock that tumbled from the rim above has lodged fast in the fork of a piñon pine tree and is slowly being grown into the trunk, wrapped in bark and time. The rock will remain suspended there, practically in mid-air, until the tree dies and falls over, and then the rock will continue on its way. It also makes us think about looking up once in a while for falling rocks. When we reach the layer of Hermit Shale John sits and matches the dark red color with his paints, adding another footnote to his list of canyon textures and colors.

When we finally arrive at the Tonto Platform we find it's not nearly as flat as it looked from above. From the rim the canyon appeared in three more or less distinct stages. There were the steep, eroded cliffs and ridges of the rim leading down to the flat plain of the Tonto Platform, then another drop down into the gorge where the Colorado River runs. John makes a note to try to include the steep relief of the ridges and deep

J. Dawson

Black throated sparrow

washes in his painting. The broad expanse of the Tonto Platform is covered mostly with black-brush, spaced evenly apart and giving it the gray-green color we saw from the rim. The effect is comparable to the art technique of pointilism, or to color printing, where lots of little dots blend together, so when you step back a ways it creates a smooth color. Here and there are saltbush plants adding a lighter tone.

We see black-throated sparrows everywhere in the blackbrush. Some perch on top and others flit out practically from under our feet and disappear into another bush. Kathleen looks carefully for a sparrow nest in the blackbrush, but finds only rabbit pellets. There are several seasons' accumulation of pellets; some are bleached almost white and others are fresh and nearly black. They are mostly from desert cottontails, with maybe a few from black-tailed jackrabbits, and there are enough pellets to convince John to stop and draw a cottontail sitting here.

Out in the middle of the Tonto Platform we find a shallow wash where the Tapeats Sandstone is exposed. This is the hard rock layer that creates the Tonto by resisting erosion, and is the cause of the light brown streaks in the landscape we could see from above. The Tapeats lies in big sheets and it makes lots of flat ledges, abrupt overhangs and smooth slick-rock. We follow the wash, walking on sandstone that has been scoured and polished smooth by thousands of years worth of run-off. Just before the wash reaches the top of a band of cliffs and drops fifty or sixty feet, Kathleen picks a perfectly flat, smooth ledge for our camp. We stay up out of the path of any unexpected flash-floods and make camp. There's another ledge a few feet higher than the one we're on, and it makes a perfect table for our kitchen.

Desert Cottontail

Tonto platform campsite

Packrat nest

Under that ledge is a big pile of sticks and brush and old cactus parts where a desert woodrat, or packrat, lives. We debate the chances of having our kitchen raided during the night, but we're too tired to move on so we just hope nothing in our camp appeals to the woodrat. John peers under the rock at the fresh nest, and bets me a cold beer back on the South Rim that a packrat will be in our kitchen tonight.

With evening, a beautiful calm descends on our part of the canyon. The sun sets early for us down here at the bottom, but the rest of the canyon to our east is colored by the rich, red light of a setting desert sun. We eat a quick dinner and watch night come to the canyon. While we sit here we talk about the Anasazi, ancestors of the Hopi Indians. The Anasazi occupied the canyon about a thousand years ago. Their art, like John's, reflects the detail and texture of the surrounding country; there are animals and people and parts of things, geometric patterns that might represent the shape of the rugged land, and it reinforces our own search for texture. They never painted an overview of the canyon, no broad landscapes or big pictures.

Kathleen jokingly suggests, "Maybe they just couldn't find a big enough rock."

ANCIENT ARTISTS

WHATEVER the Grand Canyon produces, it preserves in the warm, dry climate. Dessicated wood and bleached bones spend many more years dead and dried than they ever did alive. Hardened seeds lie dormant for years, waiting for water. The outline of a primitive hand made a thousand years ago remains clearly printed on smooth rock. A shard of ancient pottery lies exposed to the elements for hundreds of years and never changes. Contrast these with the cactus blossoms that come and go, or with the fleeting memories of experiencing the canyon. Sitting on a warm rock late in the day with friends, watching the sun sink in the western sky and listening to sparrows sing good-night is about as fleeting as it gets.

The prehistoric canyon dwellers like the Anasazi didn't leave much in their passing. The art and artifacts they left behind came from the elements of the canyon: a few rock piles, pots and pieces of pots, some sketches on the rock walls and here and there a fragile bundle of sticks wound together. Their lives were the details of the canyon: seasonal seeds and nuts, trickles of water and shy desert animals. From this we try to imagine what they were like.

They didn't have geologists to interpret the rock layers and inspire them with stories of warm inland seas or ancient rivers. They weren't able to fly over the canyon in a helicopter, thousands of feet in the air, and be impressed with how big it really is. Vast expanses of space, moving land masses and epochal periods of time were unknown. Yet they found their own explanations for their incredible home. The magic of the canyon must have been even more powerful for them than it is for us.

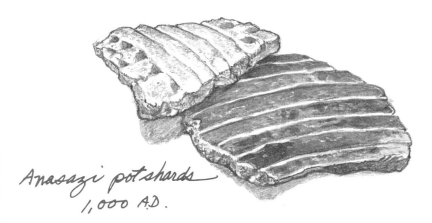

Anasazi potshards 1,000 A.D.

Archaic split-twig figurine 2,000 B.C.

The west-facing canyon walls ripen in the last red light, and then the color fades, and deep shadows take over the canyon. Black-throated sparrows sing to the evening. The moon floats up from the eastern horizon like it was untied, and it drifts up behind thin layers of cloud. A few bats appear and flitter up and down our wash. It's almost too dark to see but I can hear John's pen scratching away, drawing bats in black ink. We get in our sleeping bags and watch the night sky, thinking about woodrats, snakes, scorpions and flashfloods.

Two or three times a year snakes shed their outer layer of dried and fading skin to reveal a fresh, vivid skin beneath... Every year birds moult their feathers and grow perfect new ones... Insects shed one skin and identity to become something else... Of all the animal attributes we observe here this one is the most appealing to a middle-aged human weathering and itching in the arid Grand Canyon climate.

C.C.

Desert or Pallid Bats

Another morning comes so quietly and effortlessly. After we spend the first hour watching the bighorn sheep and the black-tailed gnatcatchers, John keeps working on his painting until he gets in all the detail he needs.

Kathleen moves over and starts to sit on a rock next to John to watch. and I hear, "Oh, no! John, your paints have spilled all over the rock!"

John starts to apologize, "I'm sorry, I…"

Then he looks and they both laugh at Kathleen's joke. The bright splashes of yellow and orange are patches of lichens growing on the rock, almost perfectly matching John's paints. His paints complement the lichen-covered sandstone so well that John does a little painting of his paint pans.

The eclipse line, the line between sunlight and shadow created by the canyon walls blocking the sun as it moves across the sky, lights up a delicate paintbrush plant. When you step into that line there's a bit of soft, diffused light that makes everything look like it's a beautiful morning. To one side is harsh sunlight and to the other is shade, but on that thin, moving line you can find enchantment all day.
C.S.

Scattered all through-out the Grand Canyon are the remains of small, pre-historic stone firepits where Ancient American Indians roasted the succulent roots of century plants for food. Other agave species provided Indians in the Southwest and Mexico with food, rope and basket fibers, soaps and poisons. Some species are fermented for drinks like pulque or tequila. Utah agaves in the Grand Canyon serve mainly as bird perches and as a sort of metronome to mark the ephemeral nature of life.

C-C.

Century plant
or Utah Agave

We pack up to start for the Colorado River, but we decide to walk around for a few hours in the wash and up a ridge, exploring the open expanse of the Tonto Platform. We find several tall Utah agave plants that have flowered and died. Like many things we've seen here, these are another reminder of the natural increments of time. The agave, or century plant, lives quietly for twenty-five years or so, and then one spring sends up a ten-foot tall flowering head, and dies. Things here seem to be either on a huge time scale or they are ephemeral, coming and going within days. On the relatively flat desert floor the agaves are a perfect place for birds like the black-throated sparrows to sit and sing.

The Tonto Platform becomes a dry oven by mid-morning and we turn our thoughts to the cold, green Colorado River hidden in the deepest gorges of the Grand Canyon. With our minds on water we pay attention to the signs of all of it that has come and gone here in the past, from gullies and washes to eroded slopes leading up to the rim rocks. We find our trail again where it enters a narrow little canyon and begins winding down beside a dry streambed toward the river below. Like all the uncountable tons of rock that had to erode to form the Grand Canyon, we also move step by step, slowly down toward the river that carried all the debris away.

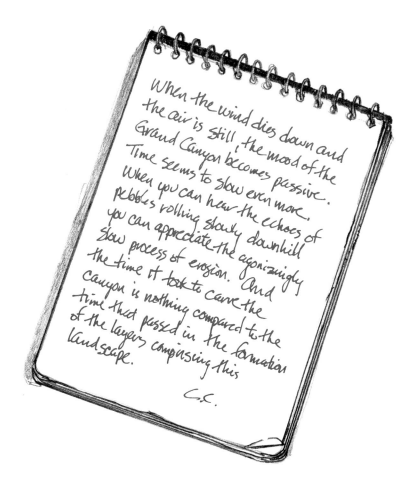

When the wind dies down and the air is still, the mood of the Grand Canyon becomes passive. Time seems to slow even more. When you can hear the echoes of pebbles rolling slowly downhill you can appreciate the agonizingly slow process of erosion. And the time it took to carve the canyon is nothing compared to the time that passed in the formation of the layers comprising this landscape.

G.S.

Watercolors

THE RIVER

COLD, green water rushes relentessly past while John and I peer down into the murky swirls, looking for a particular rainbow trout. We're lying on top of a big granite ledge a foot above river level, with our feet baking in 100-degree heat and our faces just inches from the icy Colorado River. John saw a big trout swim out from behind a submerged rock a minute ago, and now we're trying to trick it into coming after some light-colored rock chips we're throwing in the water. The chips sink and drift down past the ledge, but the rainbow isn't fooled. We think about trying to catch a beetle or caterpillar to throw in, but it's been a lazy morning so far and we'd rather lie in wait, sweating on the hot rock and whispering fishing stories.

Kathleen was waiting patiently for us to finish fooling around with the trout but now she has seen something move deep in a crevice in the rocks near her. She is hoping to see a chuckwalla, a type of big lizard. There's so much contrast between the bright sunlight and the dark crevice that the only way she can see in is to press her face close to the rock and shade her eyes, but as she does this she thinks of rattlesnakes. She decides to go sit in the shade of a nearby tamarisk and wait.

With all three of us quietly waiting and watching, the sounds of life return to the narrow band of green vegetation along the river's edge. A steady buzz of insect noise builds up and a lone hummingbird buzzes past overhead. From across the river comes the distinct slap and whistling sound of ducks taking off, and a small flock of blue-winged teal rises up from an eddy behind a rock and flies off downstream. They look tiny, and it gives us a sudden perspective of the size of the sheer rock wall across from us.

chuckwalla

Fremont Cottonwood

There's a side canyon just downstream we want to see, so we give up on the trout and the chuckwalla. The trail veers away from the river and into intense desert heat, and within minutes we're parched and looking forward to a cool swim. Our map shows a stream in the canyon.

When we enter the side canyon we wade up the trickling remains of a shallow, seasonal creek, skirting around big rocks and deeper holes. Within a few minutes we're in the shade of few small cottonwood trees that overhang the stream. There's obviously no place to swim up here unless it rains, but it's relatively cool. In this narrow canyon the hydrating effects of water are magnified by the enclosing rock walls and it feels more like a greenhouse, moist and lush. We can hardly believe that this oasis can be hidden here; from the rim it looked like just another dry, eroded crevice in the bottom of the canyon. The creek disappears under a bed of gravel laid down by years of flash-floods and we continue up the canyon on dry cobble.

When we reach a point where the rock walls close in even more, we find a seep, where water trickles out of a crack in the rock and flows slowly down the face. Moss and ferns surround the seep and there are crimson monkeyflowers and columbines growing out of the moss. A lizard clings to the rock face above the seep, waiting for flies. I can tell this is the kind of place John could spend a whole day. He sits down to draw, with his feet cooling off in a puddle of old rainwater. The more he draws the more he sees. He finds a flowering redbud tree growing from a hole in the rock near the seep, and pools of drying rainwater.

Crimson Monkeyflower

California Redbud

I see something moving in the muddy bottom of the puddle near John's feet, stirring up little clouds of silt. When I look closer I find several prehistoric-looking little invertebrates wrigggling in the mud. They're about an inch and a half long and look kind of like horseshoe crabs. We herd one over into the shallow end of the puddle where John sketches it and I take a blurry picture. We learn later these are tadpole shrimp, and their eggs may lie dormant for years waiting for enough rain to make a pool of water so they can emerge and mate once more. Like rare cactus flowers and other cyclic desert events, these little invertebrates are on their own time schedule and we feel lucky to see them.

Kathleen has gone on ahead and calls back to let us know she's reached a dead end, but that we should come see the polished rock walls. While John unloads all his art stuff in a safe spot, I scramble up over rocks and boulders to reach the next level. Kathleen is standing at the mouth of a narrow slot canyon where the stream has eroded a winding path through solid rock and worn the sides as smooth as gray marble. It's barely shoulder width and soon narrows to an impassable size. We can hear water trickling, echoing in the closed canyon somewhere up above us. John catches up and the three of us try to climb past the narrow spot, but the sculptured walls are too sheer and slick, and we have to turn around and head back to the river. John lingers momentarily at the seep, but we drag him away.

tadpole shrimp

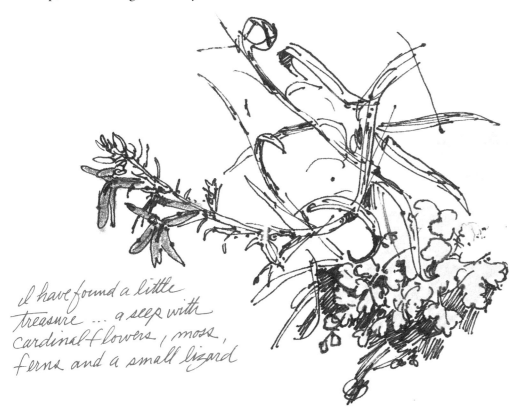

I have found a little treasure ... a seep with cardinal flowers, moss, ferns and a small lizard

Back at the river the air is warmer and breezy, but not as stifling as in the confined little side canyon. An occasional whiff of cool air comes off the river, and we sit in the shade of a tamarisk tree to eat lunch, just enjoying the contrast between the cold water and the surrounding desert. There's movement across the river, a flash of something white in the shadows along the shore, and we see a snowy egret step out of the shallow water and up onto wet sand. It looks completely out of place here, but like many birds it probably followed the river for miles and never had to experience the surrounding desert.

The regulation and clearing of the Colorado River by the Glen Canyon Dam has had other effects beside providing fish for birds like the egret. Since river flow was historically more seasonal and carried abrasive sand and silt during its raging spring floods, much of the erosion of rock has ceased. Around us we can see three forms of rock sculpted by the power of the river over many thousands of years: there are rocks fluted by the river up high on the banks where flood waters no longer touch them; there are rocks near the high water line that receive periodic scouring; and there are those imbedded in the river that only reveal themselves at times of low water. We marvel at the slow, persistent power of erosion on hard rock.

Fluting — eroded grooves and scallops record the imperceptible tempo of the river, the faintest pulse of life in the humming water. Sheet music etched in rock — A metamorphic symphony.

— CC

46...*The Grand Canyon*

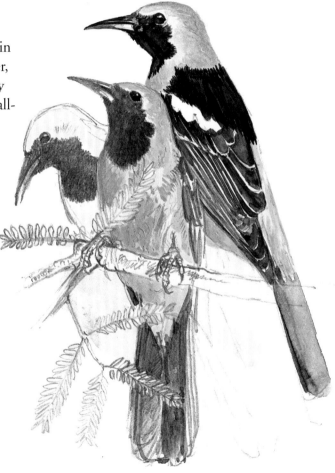

tiny trails crisscross the sand .. looks like it was a busy night.

Kathleen remarks on how the river actually has a very limited effect on the types of flora in the canyon. There are tamarisk trees and reeds growing where their roots can reach the river water, but then only a few feet away we see mesquite trees, cat's claw and barrel cactus. We pick our way along the river's edge, moving from tamarisk to mesquite and back again. I hear a Say's phoebe calling from somewhere in the tamarisk and John sees a colorful hooded oriole. In the smooth sand near the river we find all sorts of tracks. Some look like rodent tracks and others like lizard tracks. There are tiny trails left by some unidentified insects or scorpions crawling around in the night. We see where a desert bighorn sheep has come for water. John keeps busy drawing everything and our walk stalls, so I find a flat spot in the shade of a tamarisk and lie down to

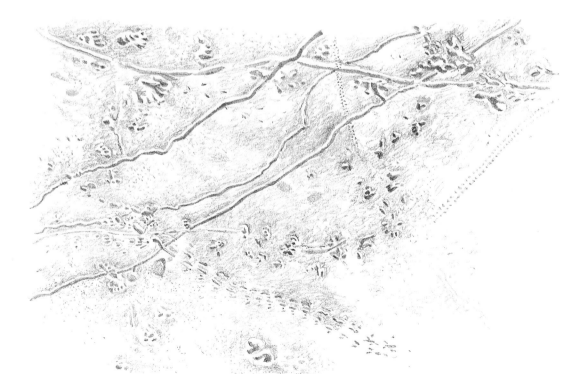

Hooded Oriole

The Tarantula hawk is a lethal looking solitary wasp. but are usually not aggressive towards humans.

listen to the mid-afternoon sounds: the river with its variety of hisses, gurgles, splashes, distant and muted roars; cicada-like insects and flies in the vegetation above me; the almost illusional, echoing sounds that seem to arrive like mirages from other parts of the canyon, rocks falling, voices, water.

A loud, almost angry buzzing makes me sit up and look, and I see a huge wasp, a tarantula hawk, circling the space where I'm resting. It looks big and lethal enough to kill me, but it lands in the sand ten feet away, rapidly flicking its wings and looking into several holes for spiders and then it flies off. After it leaves I go back to enjoying the afternoon mood until John finishes and we walk back to camp.

Sunset this deep in the canyon usually consists of just a few minutes of color in the sky overhead and then a blue-gray dusk begins. We are already so deep in shadows we can't see the rim or higher rock layers. There's a radiant, sunburned feeling to the rocks this time of day. Heat pours out of them for hours and won't let us even think about sleep, so we sit beside the river in a cool layer of air and watch it get dark.

This is a peaceful time along the Colorado River, just the promise of starlight and moonlight and with no lights of civilization flicking on. There is nothing to call wind, but the air is moving and shifting in little currents. A few bats begin to appear up and down the river, erratic shapes fluttering low over the water and circling high up over the tamarisks. We don't even try to determine what species they are. The last bit of skylight is reflected in the river, and in this we see a flat, dark head making a wake in the calm surface of a big backwater near us. It's a beaver swimming dowstream to feed on willows and tamarisk shoots. It reminds us again of all the nocturnal life that we seldom see, and some, like the beaver, that we don't expect.

Once it's completely dark and we can no longer tell river from rock, we use our flashlights to walk back up to camp. Kathleen's bright light picks up a movement near our packs and we hear a clatter and see two pairs of bright eyes reflected. Ringtails. They've been snooping in our packs and dragging out our food. They run off when we approach, but they only go to some nearby rocks and sit calmly to watch us. We secure everything, then crawl in to bed and wait for them to return. We hope they'll give up and go off to hunt for mice or insects, but soon we hear them scratching at our packs again. John's flashlight catches one in a pose on a rock.

I offer to hold the light so he can draw but he says, "I'm too tired. I can do it in the morning from memory..." and he's asleep.

J. Dawson

THE BALD EAGLE

SITTING beside the stone-and-mud Anasazi granary high above the river at Nankoweap Creek, John and I enjoy one of the classic views in the Grand Canyon. Across from us is a big, sweeping bend in the river with a massive expanse of Redwall Limestone that gently curves with the river, and downstream is a spectacular three-mile-long straight stretch of river and open canyon. Below us is the Nankoweap Creek delta where the Anasazi grew the corn that was stored here in the granary. I sit and watch ravens and swifts and I describe for John a bizarre scene.

One day in mid-winter in the canyon, a bald eagle appears in the desert sky over the rim and glides down to Nankoweap Creek, then another eagle lands, and another. The next day more eagles arrive. Soon there are twenty or so bald eagles perched on the rocks, standing in the shallow water of the creek and gliding low over the riffles. A few eagles soar in big circles out over the river, banking in wide turns next to the red rock and swooping in to land. They are here for the scores of fat rainbow trout that crowd together to swim up the creek, and many flopping trout are pulled out of the water and devoured by the eagles. Ravens sit on the rocks and watch, hopping down to grab the leftovers.

This goes on for a month or so, but eventually the trout end their run up the creek and the eagles leave as they came, one by one. The ravens hang around for a while to pick up the last of the fish remains and then they go back to normal canyon life. It will be their mating season soon.

How did the bald eagles find this brief event? There are eagles migrating through the region, but it is still a stretch from one bird stumbling upon the spawning trout to twenty-five determined bald eagles. Obviously there is some kind of communication going on, and John and I decide that the ravens started it. They have been known to attract predators to food sources they can't reach in order to get what they can in spoils.

It's a curious chain of events: for a brief portion of the Grand Canyon's life, humans have been walking around in it, and eventually we get around to damming up the river. The water turns cold and runs clear, and the trout thrive and begin to reproduce in a small creek that runs into the river. Ravens announce the presence of trout; whether before or after the first one is caught by an eagle it doesn't matter, and soon there is a feast. This goes on each winter for a few years, but trout numbers in the canyon decline for unknown reasons and the eagles go elsewhere, leaving the canyon to the ravens. We humans caused all this with our dam, and we are the only witnesses and the only record of it. There will be no fossils of bald eagles and trout. There will be no Anasazi pictograph of a big bird with a white head clutching a multi-colored fish. How many interesting things like this have happened naturally in the long history of the canyon, leaving no record?

Canyon wrens awaken before we do and sing in the dark calm of very early morning. Their sweet, descending notes are the perfect alarm clock. We want to hike up one more side canyon this morning before we start for the rim, so we get up with the wrens. John quickly sketches last night's ringtails from memory and takes photographs of the rocks where they sat. The morning's temperature is pleasant after a long night of radiant heat from the rocks, but we can feel the heat being turned up again for a cloudless day.

Even the river seems quieter at this time of day. We find sacred datura blossoms still open to the night and we stop for John to photograph them. The huge white flowers will close up as soon as the sun hits them, but we find some in the shade of a big boulder that are still open after bright sunlight has surrounded them. They have a magical look to them, so big and perfectly white, and it doesn't seem surprising that they are poisonous.

Canyon wren

Costa's hummingbird

When we push through tamarisk and willow thickets to reach the river bank we startle a great blue heron out of the shallows near shore and it squawks and flies across the river and settles on a rock. John has time to sit and sketch it before the heron lifts off and flies gracefully upriver and out of sight around a bend. John draws a series of heron shapes in the various stages of take-off and flight.

We hurry on and reach the side canyon at the same time the rays of sunlight do, and we turn away from the river into a beautifully lit, open canyon. Once we pass the mouth of the canyon where a delta of rock and gravel has built up from past flooding, we find an almost park-like glade of lush, green cottonwood trees, shrubs, vines and reeds lining the creek. The water in the stream is clear and warm. We wade in the water and John peers into all the places on shore where a lizard or something might be hiding. There's a big, flat rock halfway in the water so we sit on it to wait and watch. Not a lot is moving here this morning, but we do see two Costa's hummingbirds. They twirl around above one of the trees and then circle us to inspect our bright clothing and then are gone in an instant.

Great blue heron

Our path roughly parallels the creek, but then meanders up through rock and cactus and back to the water. On one of these meanders we find a small patch of flowering prickly pear cactus in the shade of a big cottonwood. This looks like the last of the season's blooms. There are wilted yellow blossoms and a few ragged pink ones. While John sets up and paints, I keep looking around in the rocks and vegetation for signs of life. It's still early enough in the morning that some of the more nocturnal animals might not be hiding from the sun. Between the green streamside growth and the desert hillside there's a band of cat's claw and scrubby mesquite growing low to the ground. Under the twisted, dry limbs, in the old bark and dead leaves, I find a snake coiled up in the shade. I motion to Kathleen and she comes over and we lean carefully over for a closer look. It's a small rattlesnake with a definite pinkish hue to it, so we're pretty sure it's a Grand Canyon rattlesnake. John runs over when we tell him and he has plenty of time to photograph and then draw it. The snake never moves and we leave it still peacefully coiled up.

Grand Canyon rattlesnake

Prickly pear cactus

Within a quarter mile, the canyon walls close in and we're in the shade again. The sheer rock walls are so close and so high that it seems as if sunlight seldom gets in here. The stream and the trees feel crowded together by towering rock walls. Whatever we say is instantly echoed. When we reach a small pool formed by huge boulders and our path disappears, we decide it's time to turn around. John walks around the pool of water and finds almost a dozen canyon tree frogs clinging to the moist rocks at waterline. He has to balance his sketchbook on his lap while he squats in the shallow water to draw.

On the way back to camp we get sidetracked by the collection of rocks that form a small delta where this creek runs out into the river. The rocks were washed down the side canyon during flashfloods, and they represent most of the rock layers that make up the canyon. Varying shades and textures of sandstone and limestone, granite and shale lie jumbled together. We try to stack them into a small cairn in their proper Grand Canyon order, but it's a hopeless puzzle. Many pieces are missing and some we can't identify. Kathleen finds one nice piece of Kaibab Limestone, polished from its journey and revealing a dozen small fossils. They look like shells. We confidently leave it on top of our cairn to represent the rim.

It's mid-morning by the time we start packing up camp, and the early heat promises a long, parched day ahead. We agree that the late start for our hike out was worth it. Kathleen refills our waterbottles at the river and purifies the water, and while she's sitting there she sees a velvet ant, white and fuzzy, scrambling around on the sand. This will mean another delay, but she calls John over so he can see it. With the field guide we identify it as a thistledown velvet ant, actually a wasp, and we sit for half an hour while John crawls around after it. While we're sitting I tell Kathleen and John about seeing a gila monster once in the lower canyon, and my story and a gila monster drawing also end up in John's sketchbook.

Canyon tree frog

½ inch long

Thistledown Velvet-ant

Gila monster from Charlie's story

Bobcat rest area

Our hike back to the rim is long and quiet. We feel like ants laboring in the immense landscape. Whenever we stop for water and a rest we all look back down the trail and think of the cold water and shade trees we've left behind. The rim with its pine forests and cool evening breeze is still a long way off.

John's cooler is banging against his leg as we work our way up a steep set of switchbacks and he mumbles, "I'm glad we're in a national park and I had to leave all the rocks where I saw them."

When we level out and cross a small wash, John stops us and tells us about seeing a bobcat in a similar wash not far from here years ago. That's enough of an excuse for us to stop, and we get John to sit for a long rest while he draws and tells us a story of what he saw then.

We arrive at a long, exposed ridge that leads up to the last three miles or so of steep hiking. A late afternoon thunderstorm is looming over the rim and by the time we are out in the middle of the ridge it hits us with swirls of wind and blowing dust. Most of the rain evaporates before it touches ground. Lightning strikes a nearby ridge and thunder rolls away across the canyon and back, and we all walk a little quicker until we reach a rocky pinnacle that gives us a feeling of protection. The canyon air has come alive with static electricity and the scent of rain-dampened earth and a hint of wet sage. The storm rolls past and carries out over the heart of the canyon where it flickers a few times and seems to spread itself out. For a few minutes a rainbow glimmers weakly across the falling rain and then it disappears, and the last of the rain falls quietly down into the canyon. I try to imagine the entire canyon shifting downhill toward the river one tiny notch and eroding an imperceptible bit wider as the raindrops hit.

John sits with his back to a rock and sketches the phases of the storm as it looked sweeping over us and on into the canyon. We think it's a fitting good-bye from the canyon: lightning, thunder, a rainbow and then a serene, rosy sunset. We feel refreshed from the storm and push on. It seems that we are walking out of a three dimensional John Dawson painting. We make the last few turns in the trail during the quiet hour between sunset and dark, Kathleen in the lead and John with his head full of Grand Canyon details, carrying his ugly blue cooler full of fine art. I linger for a minute before going up over the top, and I watch a raven glide past below me, saying good-night.

FINISHING TOUCHES

BACK on the South Rim the next morning we sit at a long wooden table with all of John's sketches and drawings, and he transfers notes to the unfinished painting he first started a week ago. He tells us what each color and texture detail represents as he pencils them in the margin: blackbrush, sandstone, pottery shard, cottonwood leaves, ponderosa pinecone. From my notes we add times and seasons and desert cycles. My notes will blend with John's to produce field notes, the written essence of each discovery. John's vision of the Grand Canyon develops deep in his mind, with all the tiny dots and specks of color like pine nuts and harvester ants and coyote tracks, and then gradually works out through lizards and monkeyflowers until he sees cliffs of Redwall Limestone and the first clear rays of the morning sun lighting up the canyon. No one but us will see the single dot of green paint that reminds us of the hidden canyon where we lay by a clear stream in the shade of a cottonwood tree and watched hummingbirds circle a yellow prickly-pear blossom.

John and Kathleen and I walk out to the rim for a last sunset. We start by sitting together, but then we get up and wander around, and each of us find a rock and a view of our own. If I twist around and look through the limbs of a piñon pine, I can see John sitting with his sketchbook on his lap and staring off into the canyon. Kathleen is out on a point of rock with her binoculars, following the flight of a pair of ravens in the wind. I find myself ignoring the red western sky and watching, instead, the shifting light and colors deep in the canyon below.

The wind dies down and I can hear faint canyon and rim forest sounds. I feel a bit distanced from the canyon now, probably from realizing I don't know it was well as I thought. Between John's discoveries and my own, I've just revealed more unexplored side canyons, more things to learn. I get restless and go back to see if John is drawing, and find Kathleen already there. We sit until the canyon darkens in shadow and the tops of big clouds to the east catch the last faint color of the day.

On the next viewpoint to the west I can see a family of tourists leaning over the handrail to peer down into the canyon. For them this canyon is just a vast and improbably beautiful place, and for a moment I envy the simplicity of their enjoyment. But I think it's a human trait to want to know what makes things the way they are. I've been shown the Grand Canyon from the point of view of geologists, botanists, historians and biologists. And now, like the successive layers of deposition that built this landscape and created the bones of the earth, I've added another perspective to my appreciation. I've looked through an artist's eyes to see the hidden colors and the texture of details that create the perfect composition of the Grand Canyon.   *finis*

Raul Trejo: Originally from Mexico, Raul was art director for an advertising agency when he met John Dawson and they became good friends. Raul has been a freelance designer and art director for the last thirteen years. He is involved in fine arts and has had several one-man shows of his own artwork. Raul's design skills, artistic sense and friendship inspired John Dawson to think of illustrating his own books.

John D. Dawson: John worked for an advertising agency after college and then began illustrating biology and geology textbooks on his own. Since 1978 he has illustrated for a variety of national clients including Reader's Digest Books, Audubon posters, U.S. postage stamps, various national park publications, National Geographic Magazine, Golden Guides and limited edition prints for Greenwich Workshop. His illustrations are all of natural history subjects, ranging from ants to dinosaurs and from moss to giant redwood trees. Six years ago John left his home in the mountains of Idaho for Hawaii. John wonders if there is anything in nature he hasn't illustrated.

Kathleen Oshiro Dawson: Kathleen has worked as a writer, photographer, researcher and restaurant manager. She and John were married in 1976 and they have worked as a team ever since, traveling to all John's assignments where her notes, photographs and ideas have added to every one of his paintings. Somehow she dragged John away from his work long enough to learn to play tennis, which they both love and often play as a good mixed doubles team. Kathleen and John have lived in Hawaii since 1989.

Charles Craighead: Charlie has worked as a biologist, photographer, filmmaker, carpenter and writer. He has written three other books and written narration for several natural history programs for PBS. He teaches an annual photography workshop on the Colorado River in Grand Canyon, where he met John and Kathleen, and where he tricked John into stepping into a bottomless pool of water. Charlie lives in Moose, Wyoming.

Robert M. Petersen: Bob began his printing career as a "printers devil" while in grade school and, with the exception of a stint in the Air Force, has been active in the printing industry ever since. The main thrust of his efforts is nature oriented publications. He holds a degree in printing management and is president of Haggis House Publications, Inc. in Salt Lake City. Free time is spent boating and fishing.

THIS BOOK WAS PRINTED AND BOUND IN THE UNITED STATES OF AMERICA
THE STOCK IS 100# MEAD SIG-NATURE TEXT AND 100# MEAD SIG-NATURE COVER BOTH RECYCLED STOCKS MANUFACTURED BY MEAD PAPER COMPANY
THE TYPE IS ADOBE GARMOND
COLOR SEPARATIONS BY COLOR IMAGE, PRINTED BY LORRAINE PRESS AND BOUND BY MOUNTAIN STATES BINDERY
SALT LAKE CITY, UTAH, USA

The Canyon's Gift

To let us see, with a child's awe…
Freshness, where an ancient
shore seeped colors old as life.
The immensity of air, with all
its strife of ravens, mirage
and desert dust.
Where footprints turn
to sand, to stone
then, folded back in Earth's
dark crust, remain.
As many cactus spines
as years, alone, each
waiting to be touched.
In time, layers neatly set,
snared grain by grain and
trussed with strands
of fossil bone.
Desert rain, and then
the sweetest contradiction,
cactus blossoms, one by one
combust.

C.C.